A Story
of
Our God
and
Our Catholic
Religion

Dominic Tarquin

As Inspired by the Holy Spirit

ENROUTE
Make the time

En Route Books and Media, LLC
5705 Rhodes Avenue
St. Louis, MO 63109

Cover Design: TJ Burdick, OP

Image Credits: All images courtesy of Wikipedia.org.

Library of Congress Control Number: 2017957949

ISBN-10: 0-9994704-8-5
ISBN-13: 978-0-9994704-8-0

DEDICATION

I dedicate my book to the young children who are being educated in the Catholic faith.

CONTENTS

ACKNOWLEDGMENTS

Great thanks to my wife, Marge, for her comments and the editing of my book. Her strong faith has guided the development of this beautiful story of God.

PREFACE

The book *A Story of Our God and Our Catholic Religion* should be read to children in the early grades by teachers and parents.

The intent of this book is to have young children attain a firm appreciation of the faith and be better prepared to receive the sacraments of Reconciliation and Holy Communion.

It should be read one chapter at a time, followed with a period of children's questions, as well as comments by the reader. The chapters, read **one at a time in school** by teachers, should be repeated by the parents at night. This method will provide children with a clear understanding of the story through repetition of the readings, followed by a question and answer session afterward.

Also, the prayer card in the back of the book is for children to use daily at the start and the end of their day.

The Author

INTRODUCTION

Catholic children should have a basic understanding of their faith before receiving the sacraments of reconciliation and communion.

The story you are about to read will attempt to explain how the world we live in began and how the Catholic religion has evolved through the ages to what it is today. A more detailed history can be found in the bible and the catechism of the Catholic church.

So, let us begin to read the story of God, his creation and our Catholic religion.

BENJAMIN WEST (1791) THE EXPULSION OF ADAM AND EVE FROM PARADISE

CHAPTER 1

Now our God who always was, is now and always will be is a mighty and wonderful God who created Heaven and Earth and everything in it. Now because our God is ever-loving, he created men and women in his image and likeness, to live in this perfect world.

God created the first man and woman who were known as Adam and Eve, and they lived in a beautiful garden called Eden. God said that they could eat everything in the garden except anything from the Tree of Knowledge of Good and Evil.

Now, there is an evil devil named Satan who was an angel at first but chose to commit the sin of pride and fight against God. God, because He is all-loving, kept Satan alive and created a place for him called Hell, where all sinners who do not repent may also choose to go.

Adam and Eve, who were tempted by a serpent, who was the devil, ate the fruit from the Tree of Knowledge of Good and Evil. By doing this, they disobeyed God's warning and committed the first sin, called original sin. Since we are all born with original sin, God in his mercy gave us a way to remove it by the sacrament of baptism.

Adam and Eve, as a punishment for their sin, could no longer live in the Garden of Eden. They lived for a very long time and had many children. As more and more people were born, many cities and towns formed.

As time went on, a number of bad things happened. People didn't live by God's commandment to love one another. There was hatred, discrimination, slavery, hunger and abuse.

Their sins caused God to send a large flood for forty days on the Earth, and many people were destroyed. However, a man named Noah and his family built an ark and were saved because they obeyed God's commandments.

Questions/Reflection

(Use this space to write down the questions and thoughts your child has while reading.)

RAPHAEL (1515) THE MIRACULOUS DRAUGHT OF FISHES

CHAPTER 2

God, who has infinite love and patience, wants to have all his people enter Heaven, so he sent his only begotten son to forgive sins and lead all souls home. Jesus was conceived by the Holy Spirit (the Third Person of the Blessed Trinity) and born of the Virgin Mary who was the wife of Joseph, a carpenter.

Jesus, who was to become the savior of the world, was born in a stable because there was no room at the inn. Ever since Jesus was born, he was considered a threat to the King and religious leaders because he was called the King of the Jews.

Jesus, however, who was born poor and suffered all through his life, was an example of respect and obedience to his almighty father.

Jesus lived with his parents for 30 years learning about life, woodworking and the Jewish religion. Now ready to start a new life, Jesus left home to find companions for his new adventure.

Walking along the sea shore, Jesus saw fishermen tending to their nets after they caught a good number of fish. He spoke to a man named Simon and his brother Andrew. Jesus said to them, "Come with me and I will make you fishers of men."

They left their nets and other men and followed him. Along the walk, Jesus saw James and his brother John. They, too, left their father and followed him.

From there, Jesus and his disciples traveled to villages curing the sick, forgiving sins and preaching the faith. All through his ministry, Jesus gathered more disciples and told many parables, or stories, to ever-growing crowds of believers.

Many miracles were also performed during his talk, and more and more people continued to follow Jesus. He came not to change the law but to confirm the law. Jesus said that he was not there to be served but to serve.

Questions/Reflection

(Use this space to write down the questions and thoughts your child has while reading.)

HENDRICK TER BRUGGHEN (1624-25) THE CRUCIFIXION WITH THE VIRGIN AND
SAINT JOHN

CHAPTER 3

The growing popularity of Jesus made the people happy but caused much concern among the Jewish Scribes and Pharisees, and they began to plot against him.

They decided that Jesus must be stopped, so they began to find a way to put him to death.

On his way to Jerusalem, for the feast of the Passover, the people praised Jesus with palm branches and sang hosannas.

Jesus celebrated the Feast of Passover with the disciples at dinner in the upper room in the city. While they ate, Jesus took bread in his hands, blessed it, broke it and said, "Take and eat, it is my body."

Then he took the cup, gave thanks and gave it to them, saying, "This is my blood which will be shed for many."

After the dinner, they went out to the Mount of Olives and came to a place named Gethsemane to pray.

Then, Judas, one of the twelve, led a group of the Chief Priests, Scribes and Elders and identified Jesus to them for 30 pieces of silver.

They seized Jesus and took him to the high priest Caiaphas where he was questioned and accused of blasphemy.

They found Jesus guilty and handed him over to Pilate who found no fault with Jesus but fearing a revolt by the Jews kept Jesus and released a prisoner named Barabbas.

The guards tortured Jesus, had him carry a cross to Golgotha where he was crucified along with two other men. Jesus suffered for three hours after being nailed to the cross.

Jesus accepted this unbelievable death for the forgiveness of all our sins.

Questions/Reflection
(Use this space to write down the questions and thoughts your child has while reading.)

DUCCIO DI BUONINSEGNA (1308-11) APPEARANCE BEHIND LOCKED DOORS

CHAPTER 4

After Jesus died on the cross, he was taken down and placed in a tomb.

When the Sabbath was over, Mary Magdalene and the other Mary went to the tomb with spices to anoint Jesus.

When they arrived, they found the tomb was open and a young man, clothed in white who said, "Do not be afraid. Jesus of Nazareth has been raised. He is not here."

Later that day, Jesus appeared to the disciples, although the doors were locked, and stood in their midst and said to them, "Peace be with you, as the Father has sent me, so I send you."

When he had said this, he breathed on them and said,

"Receive the Holy Spirit. Whose sins you forgive are forgiven them, and whose sins you retain are retained."

Thomas, one of the twelve, was not with them when Jesus came. So, the other disciples said to him, "We have seen the Lord."

But he said to them, "Unless I see the mark of the nails in his hands and put my finger into the nail marks and put my hand into his side, I will not believe."

Now a week later his disciples were again inside and Thomas was with them. Jesus came, although the doors were locked and stood in their midst and said, "Peace be with you."

Then he said to Thomas, "Put your finger here and see my hands and bring your hand and put it into my side and be not unbelieving but believe."

Thomas answered and said to him, "My Lord and my God."

Jesus said, "Have you come to believe because you have seen me? Blessed are those who have not seen and have believed."

Questions/Reflection

(Use this space to write down the questions and thoughts your child has while reading.)

PIETRO PERUGINO (1495-1498) THE ASCENSION

CHAPTER 5

Jesus appeared to the disciples at other times and worked miracles as a means of reinforcing their faith in him.

He said to them, "These are my words that I spoke to you while I was with you, that everything written about me in the Law of Moses and the Prophets and Psalms must be fulfilled."

Then, the Lord Jesus, after he spoke to them, was taken up into Heaven and took his seat at the right hand of God.

Before he ascended, Jesus gave instruction through the Holy Spirit to the Apostles whom he had chosen.

When the time for Pentecost was fulfilled, they were all in one place together.

Suddenly, there came from the sky a noise like a great driving wind, and it filled the entire house.

Then, there appeared to them tongues as of fire, which parted and came to rest on each one of them and they were all filled with the Holy Spirit and began to speak in different tongues as the Spirit enabled them to proclaim.

The disciples went forth and preached everywhere the proclamation of eternal salvation.

Many people in the various lands heard the preaching by the Apostles and were converted to the Christian faith.

Questions/Reflection

(Use this space to write down the questions and thoughts your child has while reading.)

SAINT JOSEPH CATHOLIC CHURCH (WAPAKONETA, OHIO, 2016) STAINED GLASS

Chapter 6

Since Jesus Christ lived, died, rose from the dead and ascended into Heaven over 2,000 years ago, many things have taken place that have resulted in the bible, the mass, the Catholic church/religion and its organization as know it today.

The most important tradition that Jesus Christ instituted during the Passover meal at the Last Supper is the Holy Eucharist which is celebrated at every Catholic mass.

They Holy Eucharist is the transformation of the bread and wine into the body and blood of Jesus Christ.

In order to be able to receive the Holy Eucharist, we must first be in a state of grace and free from sin by confessing our sins to the Priest.

When we eat this body and drink this blood, which has been transformed from the bread and wine by the Priest, we have Jesus Christ living in us.

That is why it is important for us to be free of sin and to be like Jesus Christ in all that we do and say.

To be good, practicing Catholics, we must make a sincere confession, attend Mass, receive the Holy Eucharist and pray daily.

All of this will help us to resist temptation and be faithful to our Lord Jesus Christ.

(Most Catholic churches provide mass guideline books for young children to use that explains the procedure and traditions that the priests follow.)

Our God created us, loves us forever and blesses us every day of our lives.

Thanks be to God.

Questions/Reflection
(Use this space to write down the questions and thoughts your child has while reading.)

The

End

of

the

Beginning

MORNING PRAYER

Good Morning Jesus (while kneeling)

• Thank you for my good night's sleep

• What do you want me to do for you today?

• Help me to be kind to all people I meet

• I will do my best today and every day

• I pray every day for peace in the world

• Keep me and my family safe and well today

Our Father...

NIGHT PRAYER

Good Night Jesus (while kneeling)

- Thank you for all you did for me today

- Please help all the sick people I pray for

- I'm sorry if I offended anyone today

- Please bless me and my family

- I love you Jesus with all my heart

- Keep me safe from harm while I sleep

Hail Mary...

www.ingramcontent.com/pod-product-compliance
Lightning Source LLC
LaVergne TN
LVHW072108070426 ·
835509LV00002B/73